LEARN THE VALUE OF

Giving

by Elaine P. Goley

Illustrated by Deborah Curzon Crocker

Rourke Enterprises, Inc.
Vero Beach, FL 32964

© 1989 Rourke Enterprises, Inc.

All rights reserved. No part of this book may be reproduced or utilized in any form or by any means, electronic or mechanical including photocopying, recording or by any information storage and retrieval system without permission in writing from the publisher.

Library of Congress Cataloging-in-Publication Data

Goley, Elaine P., 1949–
  Learn the value of giving.

  Summary: Suggests some ways in which one can experience the value of giving, by being generous and helping other people.
   1. Generosity—Juvenile literature.   2. Altruism—Juvenile literature.
[1. Generosity.   2. Altruism.]   I. Title.
BJ1533.G4G64   1988   88-3102
ISBN 0-86592-392-2

Giving

Do you know what **giving** is?

When you spend time with your grandma, that's **giving.**

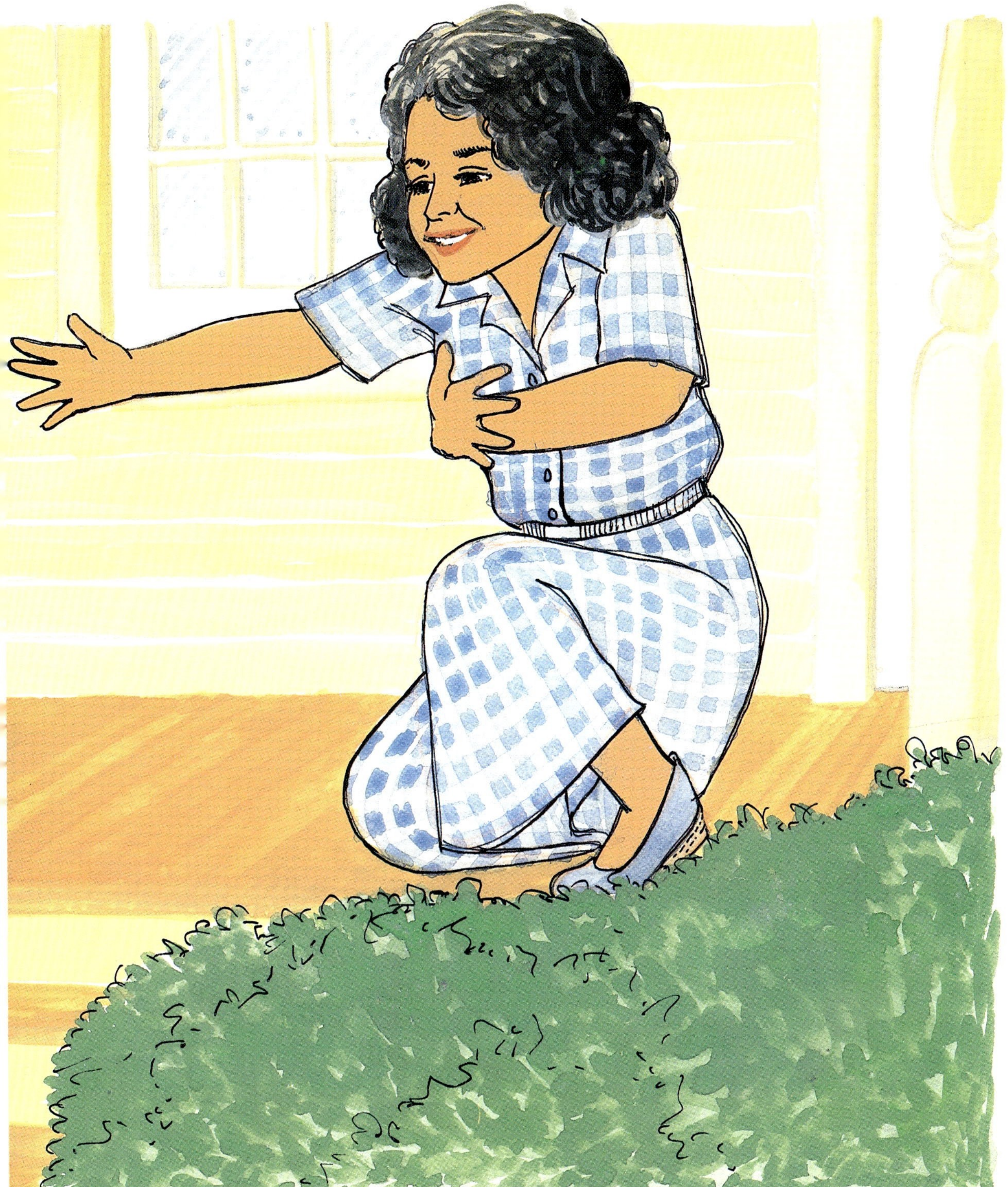

Giving is helping a friend with his homework.

Helping your mom do chores around the house is **giving.**

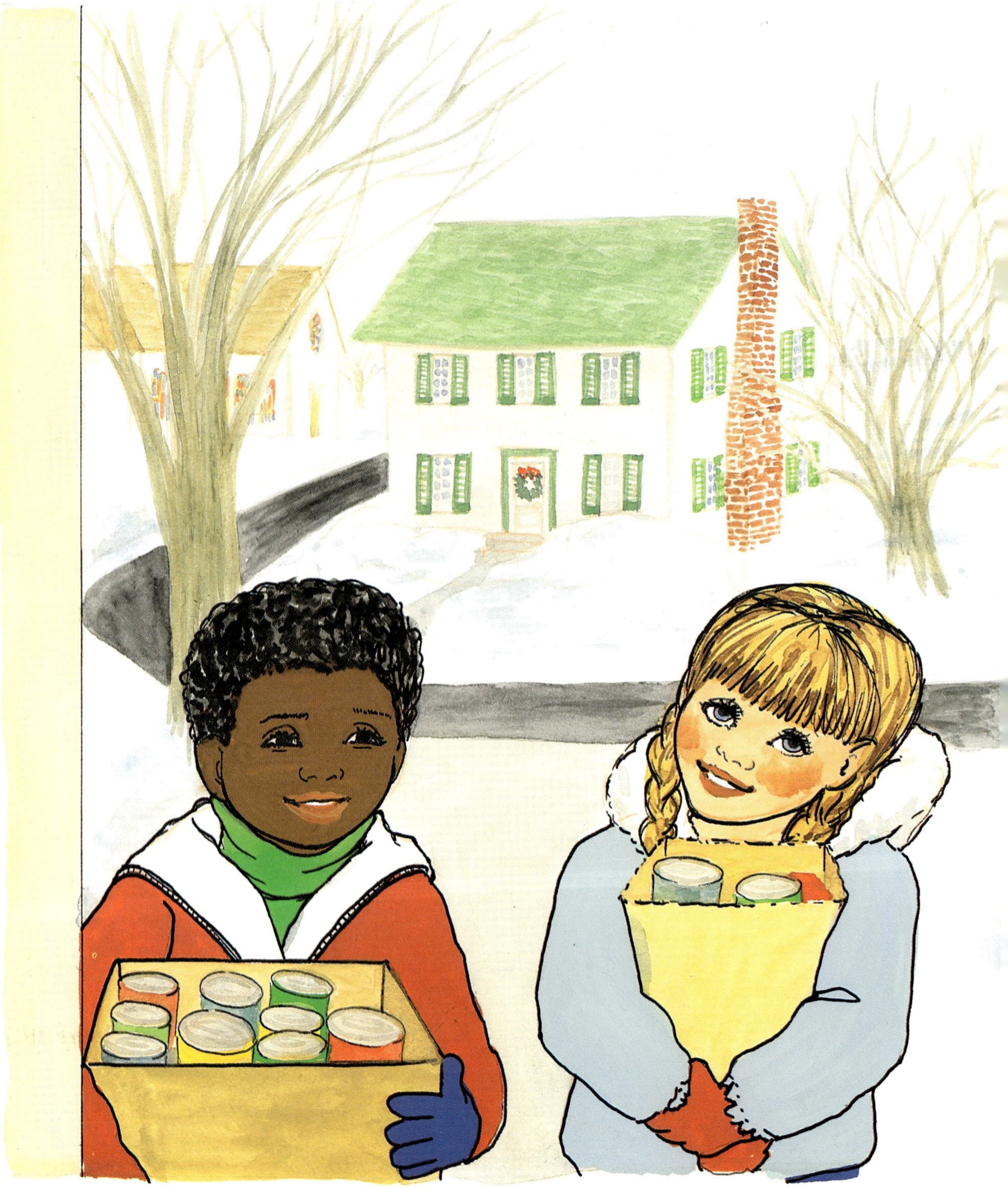

Collecting food for the needy at Christmas is **giving**.

Giving is doing an errand for your teacher.

When you read a story to your little brother, that's **giving**.

Writing a special poem for your dad is **giving.**

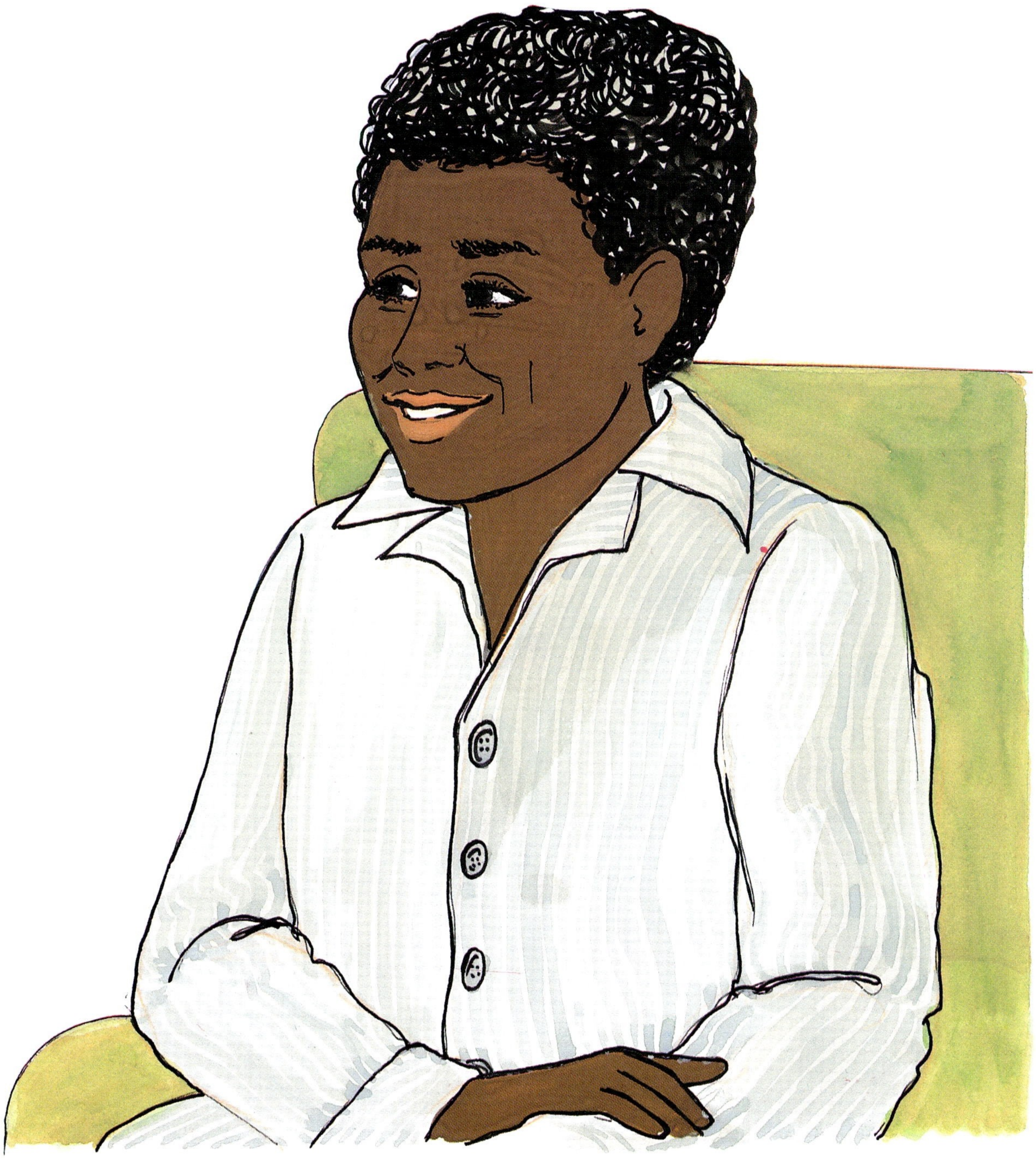

When you collect clothing for the poor, you're **giving.**

Making a Valentine for a special friend
is **giving.**

Giving is letting a friend use your pencil when he forgets to bring his to school.

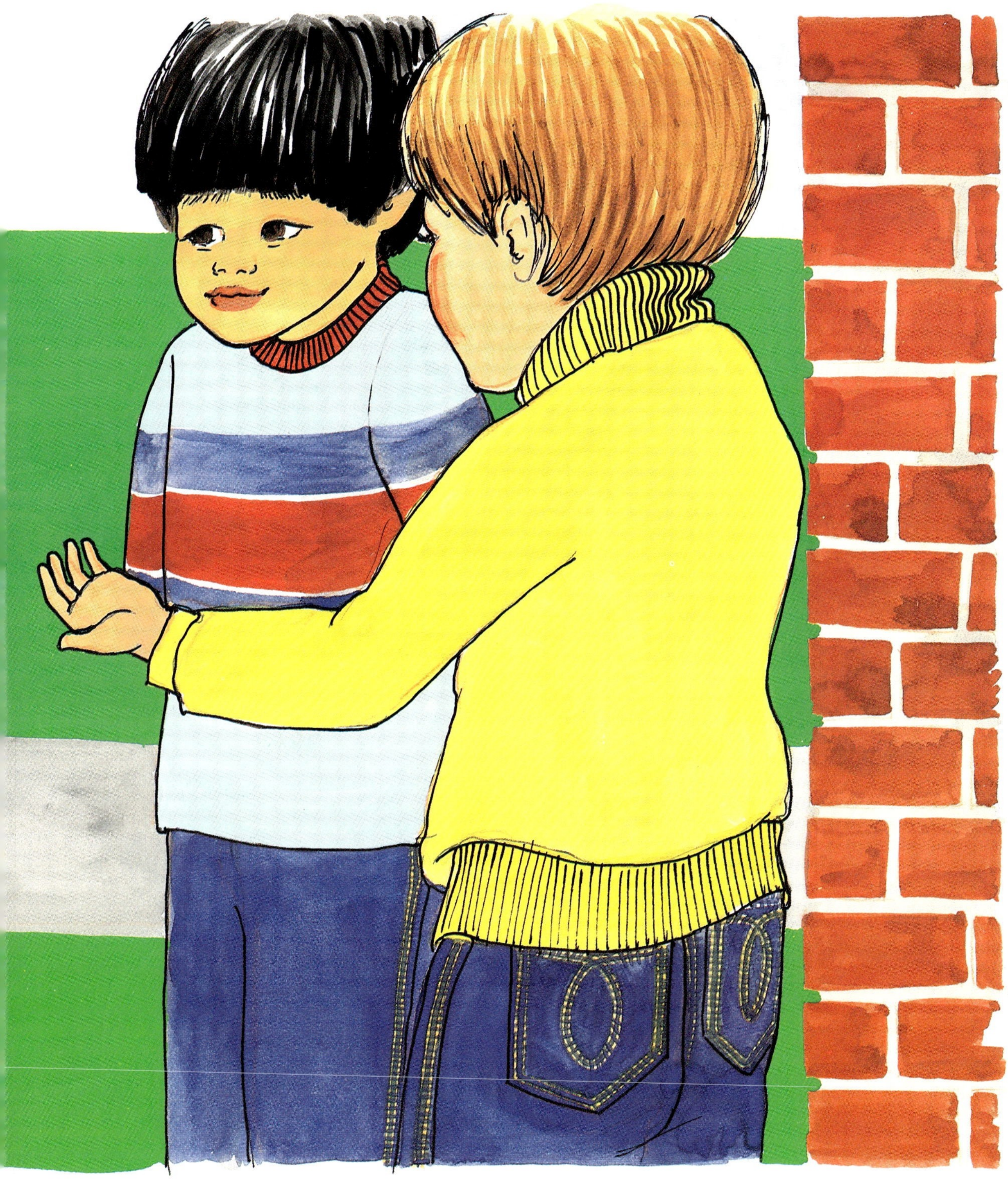

When you wash the car for Mom, that's **giving.**

Giving is helping at the school book fair.

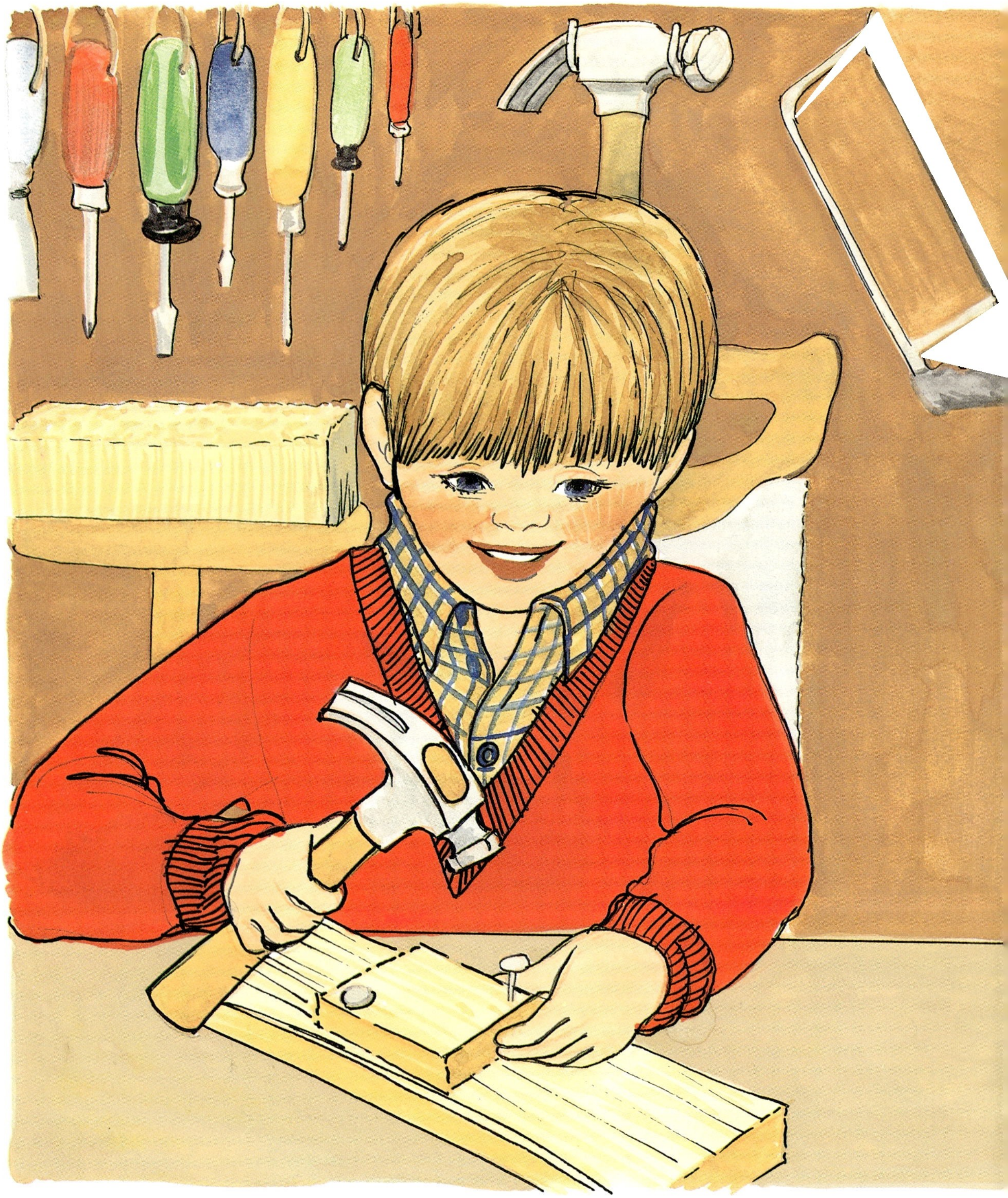

Making your dad a special present on his birthday is **giving**.

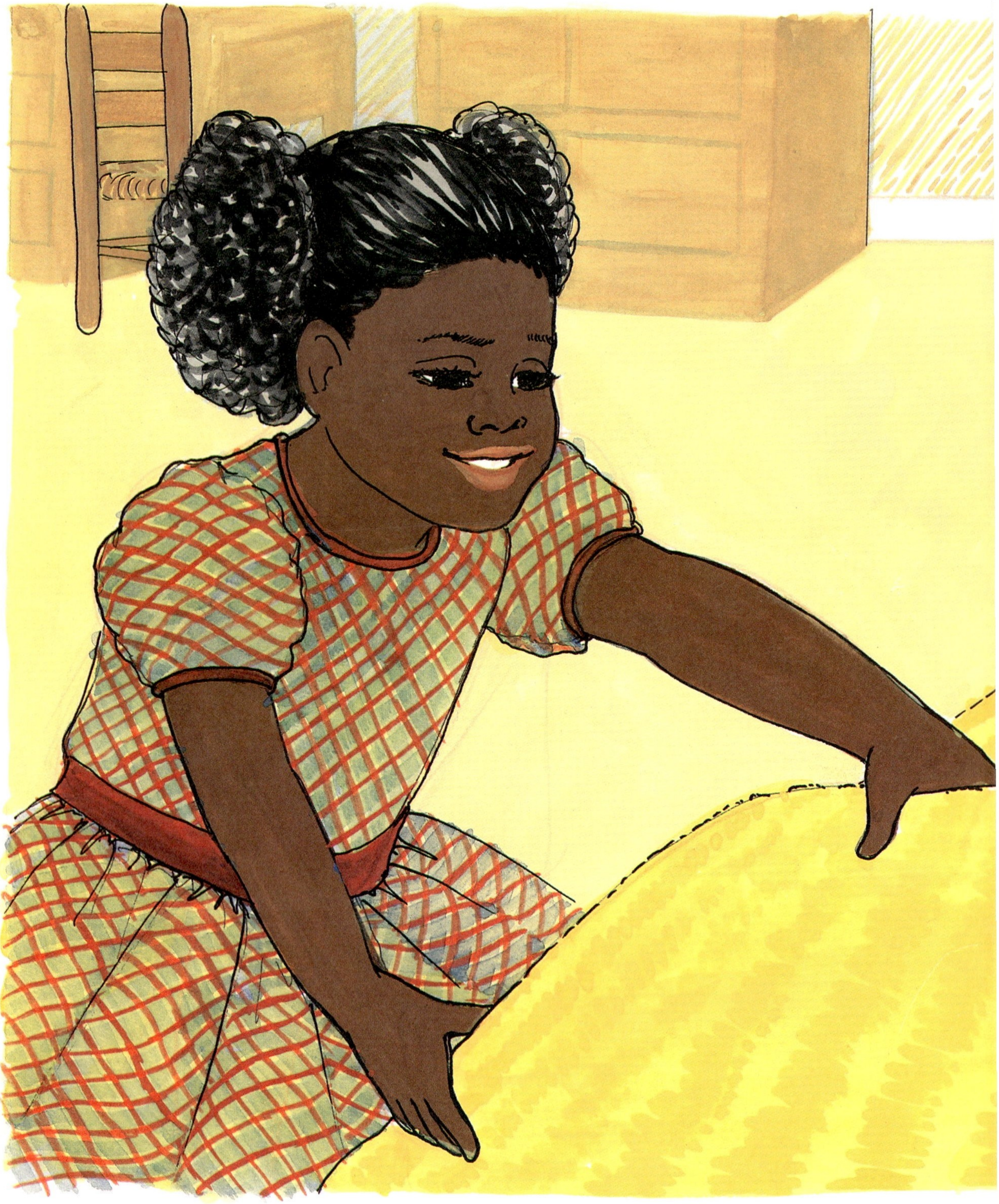

Giving is making your own bed so Mom won't have to do it.

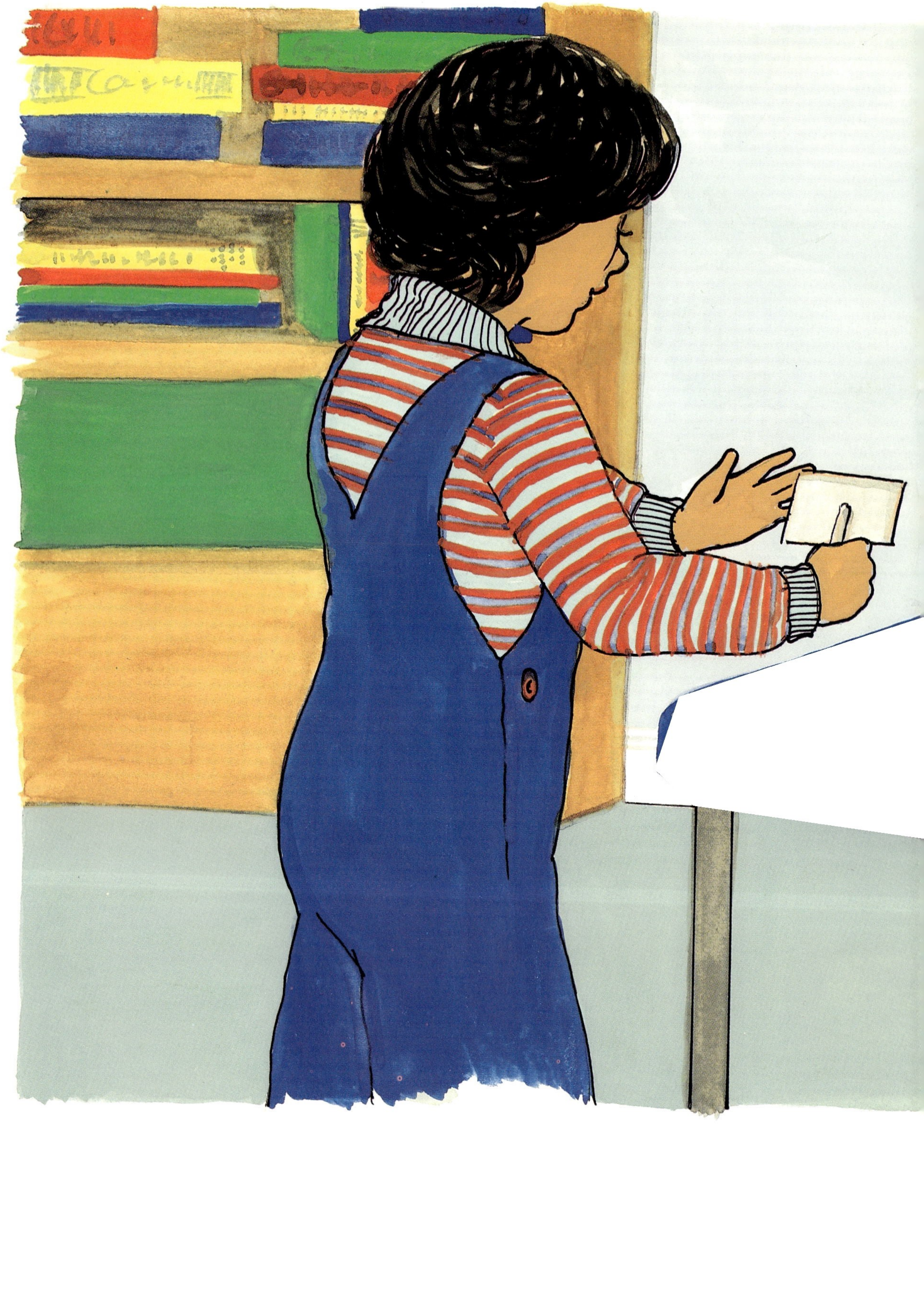

Brushing your cat so that she'll be healthy and shiny is **giving.**

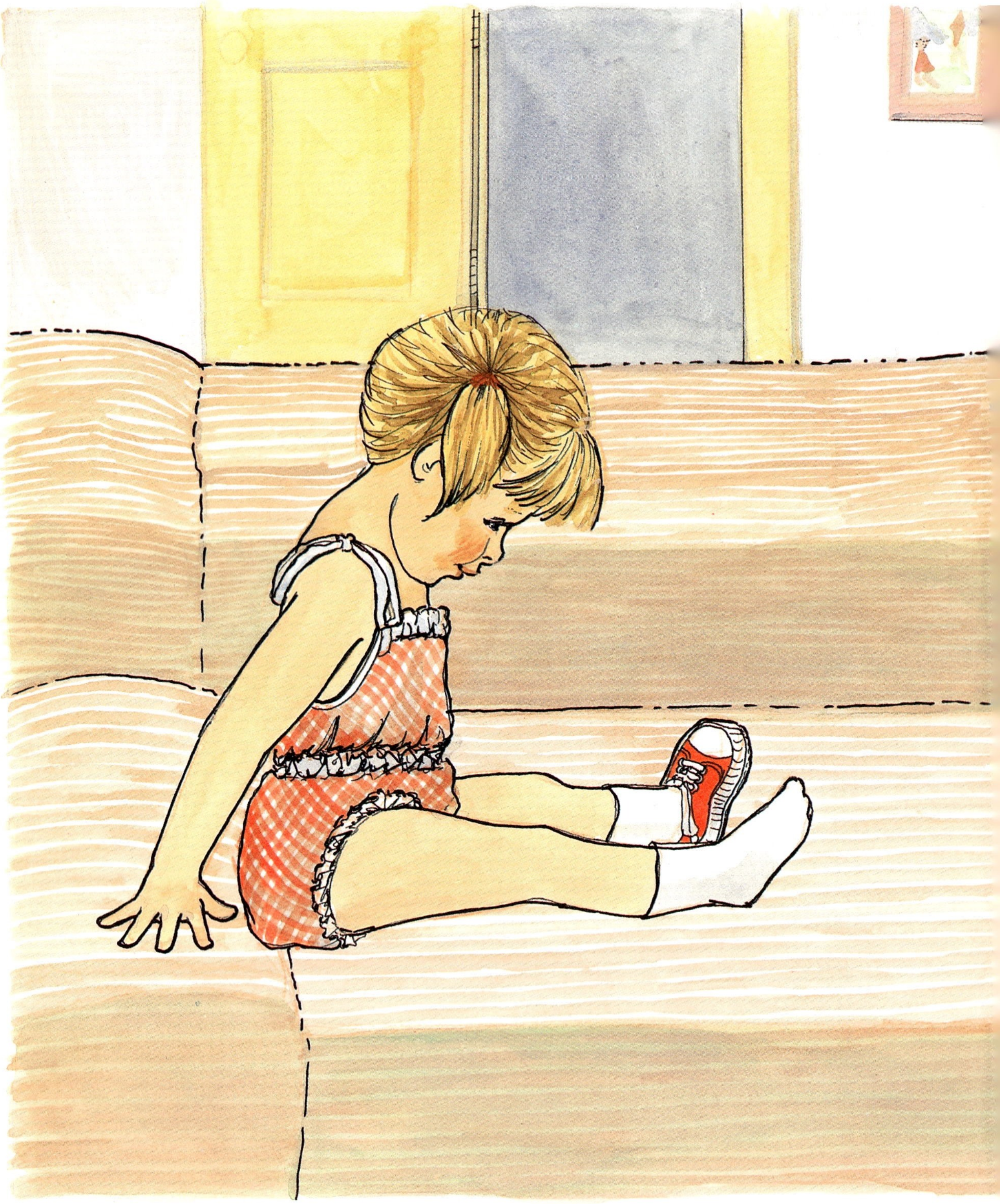

When you help your little sister get dressed, that's **giving.**

Giving is putting out sunflower seeds for the squirrels.

Giving

It was Saturday and Danny saw his friend John ride by the house on his bike.

"Hi, John," said Danny. "Tom and I are collecting newspapers today for the Cub Scout paper drive. Do you want to help?"

"No, said John, "I'm going to the park to play ball."

Danny and Tom spent the day going from door to door in the neighborhood with Tom's wagon. They asked their neighbors to donate old newspapers to the Scout's paper drive.

"The Scouts will sell the newspapers and use the money for worthwhile projects," said Danny and Tom.

By the end of the day, they had collected a lot of newspapers for the Scouts.

How did Danny and Tom show that they were **giving?**

How could John have helped by **giving?**
How could you help someone by **giving?**

Giving

Ricky and Marge had just come home from school.

"I'm going to ride my bike," said Ricky.

"I think I'll read for a while," said Marge.

"Mom will be home late from work," said Dad. "Supper will be late tonight."

The kitchen was a mess.

Ricky said, "Marge, why don't we clean up the kitchen and make a salad for supper so that Mom won't have as much to do when she gets home?"

"That's a good idea," said Marge. "I'll wash the dishes and you dry."

How did Marge and Ricky show that they are **giving** people?

How can you be **giving** at home? . . . at school? . . . with your friends?